Give Up Your Addictive Habits

Table of Contents

Foreword

Chapter 1:

Addiction Basics

Chapter 2:

Acknowledge the Addiction

Chapter 3:

Be Rational and Don't Deny

Chapter 4:

Get Coping Skills

Chapter 5:

What Are Your Triggers

Chapter 6:

Lifestyle Changes

Chapter 7:

Be Accountable

Chapter 8:

Have Support In Place

Chapter 9:

Reward Accomplishments

Terms and Conditions

LEGAL NOTICE

The Publisher has strived to be as accurate and complete as possible in the creation of this report, notwithstanding the fact that he does not warrant or represent at any time that the contents within are accurate due to the rapidly changing nature of the Internet.

While all attempts have been made to verify information provided in this publication, the Publisher assumes no responsibility for errors, omissions, or contrary interpretation of the subject matter herein. Any perceived slights of specific persons, peoples, or organizations are unintentional.

In practical advice books, like anything else in life, there are no guarantees of income made. Readers are cautioned to reply on their own judgment about their individual circumstances to act accordingly.

This book is not intended for use as a source of legal, business, accounting or financial advice. All readers are advised to seek services of competent professionals in legal, business, accounting and finance fields.

You are encouraged to print this book for easy reading.

Foreword

Imagine that you are taking a puff of a cigarette, a slug of whiskey, a snort of cocaine, a shot of heroin, a toke of marijuana. Put aside first whether the drugs are legal or not. For now, just concentrate on the chemistry. The moment you take that puff, that slug, that snort, that shot, that toke, trillions of potent molecules rush through your bloodstream before finally reaching your brain. Once they settle there, these molecules will set off a cascade of electrical and chemical events, a type of neurological chain reaction that will ricochet around your skull and rearrange your mind's interior reality. And before you know it, you are addicted.

Everyone in this world has his or her own addictions. Too much of something is bad enough and when your addictions go overboard, you should know that it is time for you to stop them before they gain full control of your system, before you reach that point of no return.

In this book, expect to learn the most effective and useful tools that can help you break free from your bad addictive habits so that you will be able to live your life to the fullest.

Chapter 1

Addiction Basics

Synopsis

Addictions are things that you need to deal with right away or else you will end up being eaten by your bad habits, and when you want to get out of their strong hold, you can no longer do anything because it is already too late.

For you to effectively stop your addictions, the most important thing that you have to do before anything else is to learn what addiction really is. By doing this, it will be easier for you to determine if what you are experiencing right now is truly an addiction or just a simple inclination to do things.

A Short Introduction to Addiction

By definition, addiction is a kind of condition that takes place when a person ingests a certain substance (e.g. cocaine, alcohol, nicotine) or engages in a particular activity (e.g. shopping, gambling, sex) that can give pleasure but the continued use or act of which can become compulsive and interfere with one's ordinary responsibilities in life, such as health, work or relationships. Users are usually not aware that their behavior is out of control and is starting to cause problems, not only for themselves but also for the people around them.

There are different types of addictions; one of them is described as physical addiction. It refers to the biological state wherein the body adapts to the presence of a drug to point that the drug no longer gives the same effect, a situation referred to as tolerance. Due to tolerance, biological reaction of withdrawal can take place when the drug has been discontinued.

Another form of physical condition is where the brain overreacts to drugs or cues related to drugs. For example, an alcoholic that walks into a bar will feel a strong pull to get a drink due to such cues.

But in most cases, the addictive behavior does not have any relation to exposure to cues or physical tolerance. There are some people who feel the compulsion to shop, gamble or use drugs as their reaction to their emotional stress, whether they have a physical condition or not. Because these kinds of psychologically based addictions are not based on brain or drug effects, people often switch their addictive actions from a certain drug to an entirely different one, or even to a non-drug behavior. Here, the addiction's focus does not matter; it is the need to do something under some form of stress. To treat this kind of condition, it is important to understand how it works psychologically.

When referring to any form of addiction, it is essential to understand that its cause might not necessarily be for the sake of searching for pleasure and that being addicted to something has nothing to do with a person's strength of character or morality.

Chapter 2

Acknowledge the Addiction

Synopsis

To finish something, you need to start with it first. The same principle applies to stopping your addictions. You can never expect to go to sleep at night and wake up the next morning with your system completely washed of your addictions when you did not do anything about it.

The first and undoubtedly most important step for curbing your addictions is to acknowledge their existence. When you accept the fact that you have an addiction, it will be much easier for you to continue on with your journey to finally setting yourself free.

Acknowledging Your Addictions – Your Initial Step to Recovery

As the old saying goes, even the longest journey starts with only a single step. The road to stopping your addictions also starts with one important step. But in the case of addiction, this is not just any step because the truth is; it is the hardest step that you might ever have to take in your life. It is a step that everyone with an addiction should take if they are truly determined to overcome their bad habits.

When you acknowledge your addiction, it means that you accept that it has become a part of your life, a part of who you are. When you have acknowledged it and you were able to face up to this difficult fact, then it is the time that you can finally start taking control, not only of your addiction but in your life as a whole. It is pretty much setting the ground rules for the upcoming battles. It is that line in the sand that marks out that start of a brand new life for you and your whole family.

Acknowledging your addiction is all about genuinely admitting to yourself, in the deepest parts of your heart, that you actually have an addiction, not just a simple problem, a serious problem that you can control if you put your mind to it.

You need to face the fact, no matter how difficult or hurtful it might be, that you have a real addiction. Of course, doing this is and will never be easy but the moment you are able to do that and you finally acknowledge it for what it really is, you will be able to own it as a part of yourself and a part of who you are.

However, it does not mean that you have to blame or hate yourself for it. It only means that you have finally decided to stop denying the reality and the excuses or justifications that are normally associated with addiction.

Chapter 3

Be Rational and Don't Deny

Synopsis

One of the most complex aspects of human natural is denying difficult truths but it is nothing to be ashamed of. This is basically a normal defense mechanism that people use when the truth becomes too difficult for them to accept.

But in the case of addicts, this denial does not protect them at all and instead, this "allows" them to continue with their addiction. That is why the second step for overcoming your addiction is to avoid denials and learning to be rational instead.

Denial: A Delusion to Overcome

When you enter the world of addiction, you will also reach a point of denial. In fact, addicts in most cases, refuse to accept any suggestion that they might have a problem. A certain study has reported that many classified alcohol or drug dependent people deny that they require treatment, while another study showed that just 1.2% out of the about 7.4 million adults in America with untreated alcohol abuse disorder thought that treatment can help them.

But why do people with addictions fail to see what other people around them see – It seems as if they have become slaves to their bad habits and that these will kill them sooner or later, know the feeling.

Denial is one way of saying that you are terrified of contemplating the real meaning of the fleeting insight that you have as far as your problem is concerned. Since you are unnerved, your brain will refuse you to let you continue to stay in denial. Denial gets rid of the need to quit and there is not anything scarier than that in the whole universe. To quit is equivalent to the world coming to an end, the end of your very self. You cannot bring yourself to imagine it, as it is like trying to project how the world would be if the laws of physics did not apply.

Even if addicts will never admit it, their rational mind does not roll over, chiseling out tiny chinks in the wall of denial. And even if their rational brain tries to battle back, denial falls back into its original position. Because addiction is a disease that continues to worsen, eventually, denial will lead to death.

Of course, this is not something that you want to happen and the best resolution is to start being rational. To stop addiction, listen to that rational voice inside your head, no matter how tiny, it is what will lead you to your recovery.

Chapter 4

Get Coping Skills

Synopsis

Coping with your addiction is the next important step that you have to take in your journey to eliminating your bad habits from your life. Humans have the innate tendency to face the things or obstacles that come their way and the same idea applies when you have been addicted to a substance or an activity. You need to cope with it so that you can emerge as an entirely different person, a person completely devoid of any bad habits.

Through these coping skills, your journey will become much easier on your part and before you know it, you will be on your way to total recovery.

Cope With Your Addiction With These Useful Skills

If you want to recover from your addiction, the first and most important rule that you have to remember is that you can never recover from it by simply stopping the habbit. Recovery will only happen if you have successfully created a life where it will be easier for you not to use. If you refuse to create a new life, then, all the factors that brought about your addiction will definitely catch up with you all over again.

However, it does not mean that you will have to change all aspects of your life and everything in it. However, there are several behaviors and things that are getting you into trouble and these will continue to cause you trouble unless you let go of them. Holding on to your old life during your recovery will make you do less.

So, what are these common coping skills that you need to develop in order to attain complete recovery from your addiction?

Stay Away from High Risk Situations

The most common high risk situations can be described by HALT, an acronym that stands for Hungry, Angry, Lonely, and Tired. While these situations cannot be completely avoided, being aware of them will help so that they will not catch you off guard, allowing you to prevent those tiny cravings from developing into major urges. Here, the best thing that you can do is take extra care of yourself. Do it by eating healthier meals, try to relax to let go of your resentments and anger, mingle with other people so you don't feel alone and improve your sleeping habits so that you will not feel tired the next day.

Practice Relaxation

There are several common reasons why some people end up using alcohol and drugs. They use these things to reward themselves, relax or escape. To put it simply, alcohol and drugs become people's way of relieving tension. As mentioned earlier, changing your life is the first rule of recovery and relaxation is not just an optional aspect but an essential part of a successful recovery. There are plenty of methods to relax. These can range from something as simple as going for a walk to those more structured methods such as meditation.

Be Honest

Addiction, most of the time, requires lying. You need to lie about the fact that you are using drugs or alcohol. Once you have developed an addiction, it will just become easy for you to lie. And when you are already good at lying, there will come a time that you will lie even to yourself. This is the reason why addicts sometimes no longer know who they are or what they believe in.

Honesty is and will always be the best policy if you want to stop your addictions. Being true to those around you and to yourself can make you go a long way towards recovery.

Chapter 5

What Are Your Triggers

Synopsis

You will not get addicted to something if nothing triggers you in the first place. An addiction is something that spurs from a certain source, for a certain reason, and one crucial step for you to stop your bad habits is knowing your triggers.

Most of the time, addicts are not aware of these triggers, that is why they find it harder to deal with their condition. They just continue to cope with their addiction without really knowing what makes them do things in the first place.

When you know your triggers, it will be much easier for you to deal and combat your addiction.

Know Your Triggers to Stop Your Bad Habits

Early on your journey to stopping your addiction, it is a good idea to take a complete inventory of all your personal triggers so that you will know the best way of handling tempting situations when they arise.

These triggers can be mental, emotional or situational and they usually come out of nowhere, catching you off guard and wrecking your desire of getting rid of your bad habits. However, by learning your triggers early on and learning how to spot those triggers that will put you at the worst risk; you can lessen your chance of being swept up again the heat of the moment.

A Glimpse to the World of Triggers

Triggers can come in different sizes and shapes. Although there are a lot of common triggers that are specifically risky for most people battling with substance abuse, there are also those personal triggers which can hold a particularly special meaning to you alone, like a date that reminds you of the lost of your loved one or another emotionally draining event. While only you will be able to assess your personal triggers and how they impact your life, it can be of great help to go through the most common triggers and come up with plans that will help you stay away from situations where they usually appear.

The most avoidable situational triggers include:

- Drug paraphernalia
- Clubs, bars and other famous drinking establishments
- Pornography

- Smoking cigarettes

- Other people that you abused substances with

- Possession of large amounts of cash

- Prescriptions for pain medications even if use is under supervision

Aside from these situational triggers, there are specific emotions that can trigger the desire of abusing substances. Frustration, depression, anxiety and anger can all prompt the urge of turning to alcohol or other substances as well as loneliness, inability to sleep and boredom.

Identifying your triggers will require you to take a personal inventory of emotions that you associate with your addiction. You need to come up with a plan of things that you can do instead of turning to alcohol or drugs. Activities such as reading a good book, calling a friend or exercising will distract you from your cravings. It can also help if you reach out to your family or friends so that you can positively cope with your emotions.

By discovering what your triggers are, it will be easier for you to develop healthy and useful strategies for avoiding and overcoming these triggers and lessening your chances of shifting your focus from your determination to stop your bad habits.

Chapter 6

Lifestyle Changes

Synopsis

Most of the time, addictions develop because of some lifestyle habits that can trigger you to do things that you are not supposed to do in the first place.

As mentioned in the previous chapters, the journey to stopping your addictions will require you to change your life for the better and when it comes to changing your life, you also need to develop different lifestyle habits to help you combat your addictions.

These lifestyle changes might look simple but they can be of great help for your addiction to be completely flushed out of your system.

Lifestyle Changes for a Better You

The benefits of lifestyle changes, like getting enough rest, changing your diet, exercising and learning how to manage your stress, have long been known to help in improving your physical health.

But do you know that these lifestyle changes can also greatly improve your mental health? According to experts, these lifestyle changes help reduce stress and anxiety, boost your mood and improve your overall wellbeing, all of which can do wonders for you to completely get rid of your bad habits.

Lifestyle changes, though they may look simple, are actually powerful tools to treat your addictions.

Dietary Changes

You need to follow a diet that is rich in whole grains and low in saturated fats. Fresh vegetables and fruits are also essential to reduce the risks of diabetes, obesity, heart disease as well as other physical health issues. Foods that have high content of omega 3 fatty acids are also discovered to improve memory and learning in adults aside from reducing symptoms of mood disorders and depression. By eating healthy foods, both your body and mind will be in good condition, which will help for you to be free of any negative emotions and sicknesses that can cause depression, which happens to be one of the reasons why some people become addicted to substances and bad habits.

Get Enough Sleep

Sleep has a very strong effect on a person's mood. When you feel depressed and do not get adequate sleep, your symptoms of depression can become worse. Fatigue, sadness, moodiness and irritability are also caused by sleep deprivation. See to it that you always get enough sleep every night so that all your body systems will function properly.

Stress Management/Relaxation

A little stress is okay but when it is too much, you know that you are in for some trouble. Practice useful relaxation and meditation techniques that can help lower your stress levels, reduce anxiety and help you unwind.

Exercise

With regular exercise, you can stay both physically and mentally fit. This will help improve your mood and help you sleep and increase your strength and energy.

During an exercise, your body releases endorphins to your bloodstream that serve as natural pain killers. Endorphins can improve your mood, making you feel good about yourself and the world around you. Exercise also lessens the level of cortisol, or the depression or stress hormone in your bloodstream.

All of these lifestyle changes are simple but can really go a long way for you to stop your bad habits in more ways than one.

Chapter 7

Be Accountable

Synopsis

Every action that you make is your own decision and your own doing. Unless you have been forced into your addiction, being addicted to something is a choice that you made. Refusing to stand up to your choices and accept that you made them in the first place will never get you anywhere.

In the same way that denial will not help, not holding responsibility for the things that you do will only make it even harder for you to stop your addictions.

Be accountable for your actions, your choices, and decisions. Be accountable for your whole life and recovery will follow.

Breaking Free of Your Bad Habits Requires Accountability

Without accountability, you will never be successful with your recovery from your addictions. A primary aspect of active addiction is the attempt to make the people around you that you are not using use. Many addicts take on an expertise to make it look as if everything is going well while simultaneously avoiding the responsibilities, consequences and just choosing to live in denial.

Part of making healthy changes is starting to lead a responsible and honest life. Being accountable for your past, present and future is a major step in you completely recovering from your addictions.

Accountability comes with multiple facets and it starts with accepting your responsibility for everything that has happened in the past.

Playing the victim is one tough habit to let go of that most recovering addicts will be able to relate to. It is just all too easy for you to put the blame on other people for what happened to you instead of accepting the responsibility for the actions that you made. At the end of the day, you have to accept that the choices made in the past are all of your doing. It is impossible to learn from your past mistakes if you will not be accountable for them. However, it does not mean that you have to feel ashamed or beat yourself up for what you did. Everyone makes mistakes but you can take a major step forward if you will accept responsibility for the bad choices that you made.

To stop your bad habits, you need to be accountable for yourself. Addiction can destroy several aspects of your life, including your body, mind and spirit. Recovery gives you the chance of healing all of your past wounds. You have to take care of yourself by including day to day responsibilities like the way you eat, the way you react to people around you and the way you think. This will also mean setting up a more positive future for yourself through creating good goals and actively improving how you look at life in general. Recovery is your best chance of living the life that you are meant to live so you better make the most of it.

Remember: you are the only one accountable for your actions and your life. By holding yourself accountable for your past and your progress to recovery, you will be able to take a gigantic step towards leading a healthier and more balanced life.

Chapter 8

Have Support in Place

Synopsis

In the previous chapter, you learned that you need to be accountable for your life and the decisions and choices that you made in the past. But, holding yourself accountable can be very difficult without the help of other people.

For this reason, you need to have support so that it will be easier for you to stay accountable for your life. You must never feel afraid of reaching out to your family and close friends who are supportive of your desire to finally stop your addiction.

With a solid support in place, it will be much easier for you to face the remaining steps that you need to take to complete recovery.

Support Groups – An Assurance That You are Not Alone in the Fight Against Addiction

If you will look closely, you will find different support groups for all situations under the sun. Support groups for divorcees, cancer patients, parents and those who have lost a loved one are all made available today. The main reason why these support groups are popular is the simple fact that they are truly helpful. You can accomplish a lot of things by just talking about how a certain situation makes you feel, especially when you know that there are other people who feel the same way.

Different Types of Support Groups

Right now, there are plenty of support groups for addiction and many of these are recommended by professionals through the years. Some groups are for those who are abuse substances. There are also those who have alcohol addiction, while other groups are for families of the addicts, for those loved ones left behind after the fatal overdose of their addict family member. There are support groups focusing on addiction to specific kinds or drugs or those that live in particular locations or those with certain professions. You can also find support groups for other forms of addiction like shopping, sex and internet addictions.

Benefits of Support Groups

You can never underestimate the power of having support groups to help you in your journey against your addiction. When a person with an addiction realizes that he is not the only person with this problem and that there are still many others who are in the same situation, it will be easier for him to take responsibility for his addiction and be more open to treatment.

Emotional support that comes from the group members can also play a big role in continued sobriety and complete recovery. Another remarkable benefit of these support groups is the "helping helps the helper" mentality. Those who choose to give their energy and time to help others that deal with a similar problem usually see great benefits. By not just receiving support but at the same time giving it to other members, you will more involved and gain more from the experience of being in the group.

Get Unconditional Support from Your Family and Friends

But aside from these support groups, the best and undoubtedly most powerful support that you can ever get is the one that comes from those people that you love, and these are none other than your family and closest friends. Instead of pushing them away when they try to help, use their unconditional love and care to serve as your inspiration to become a changed person.

Chapter 9

Reward Accomplishments

Synopsis

Life becomes more worth living when you know that for every good thing that you did, a reward is bound to come your way. By this time, you already know that stopping your addictions is possible only if you will really put your heart and mind to it.

The last but definitely not the least tool for you to completely free yourself from your bad habits is learning to reward yourself for every accomplishment that you make.

Through meaningful rewards, you can be more motivated to do better the next day and you will strive even harder to make sure that you will get another great reward in the future. With this kind of inspiration and motivation, you will have the drive to become better and better every day as you finish your journey to complete recovery from your addiction.

Every Accomplishment Deserves a Good Reward

Reward systems are being used in many situations today. At home, in schools and even in workplaces, a reward system is considered as a helpful tool for people to do better.

This serves as a motivation for the children to do their chores at home. Students learn to embrace their lessons better and complete their homework because they know that they will be rewarded for everything that they do. Employees feel more valued and appreciated when their employees reward them for their achievements.

Reward systems can certainly do wonders when it comes to inspiring people to strive better and even in your recovery from addiction, rewarding yourself for every accomplishment that you make can inspire you to move forward and finish what you have started.

Maybe you were able to say no to your friends' invitation of going to the bar after work. Maybe the sight of marijuana no longer made you feel any cravings to take a toke. Maybe you were able to stop yourself from watching the porn video that popped up during your search. These things might seem like a simple accomplishment for others but for those who are addicted to alcohol, marijuana and pornography, these simple actions are a giant leap on their way to recovery and these things definitely deserve some reward.

The rewards will be all up to. You can either set it for yourself or you can ask your family and friends to give you something for every accomplishment that you make. The main point here is that you will get something good out of being able to resist the lure of your addictions.

At the end of the day, it is not really the reward that matters. What matters is that even if there is no reward, it will now be easier for you to say No to your addictions. This is because you have already accepted it in your heart and mind that your bad habits will never do you any good and letting them go is the only way for you to be able to live the kind of life that you want, the life that you deserve.

Hopefully, this book has helped you in learning how to stop your addictions. Use the tools that you discovered to finally break free from all your bad habits.

www.ingramcontent.com/pod-product-compliance
Lightning Source LLC
LaVergne TN
LVHW020741090526
838202LV00057BA/6176